AMAZING
SCIENCE

Gusts and Gales
A Book About Wind

by **Josepha Sherman**   illustrated by **Omarr Wesley**

Thanks to our advisers for their expertise, research, knowledge, and advice:

Mark W. Seeley, Ph.D., Professor of Meteorology and Climatology
Department of Soil, Water, and Climate
University of Minnesota, St. Paul

Mike Graf, M.A., Instructor of Child Development
Chico (California) State University

Susan Kesselring, M.A., Literacy Educator
Rosemount-Apple Valley-Eagan (Minnesota) School District

PICTURE WINDOW BOOKS
Minneapolis, Minnesota

Managing Editor: Bob Temple
Creative Director: Terri Foley
Editors: Sara E. Hoffmann, Michael Dahl
Editorial Adviser: Andrea Cascardi
Copy Editor: Laurie Kahn
Designer: Nathan Gassman
Page production: Picture Window Books
The illustrations in this book were rendered digitally.

Picture Window Books
1710 Roe Crest Drive
North Mankato, MN 56003
www.capstonepub.com

Library of Congress Cataloging-in-Publication Data
Sherman, Josepha.
Gusts and gales: a book about wind / by Josepha Sherman ;
illustrated by Omarr Wesley.
v. cm. — (Amazing science)
Includes bibliographical references and index.
Contents: How wind begins—Warm and cool air—Global winds—
Local winds—Beach breeze—Hurricanes and tornadoes—Ride the wind.
ISBN 978-1-4048-0094-6 (hardcover)
ISBN 978-1-4048-0338-1 (paperback)
1. Winds–Juvenile literature. [1. Winds.]
I. Wesley, Omarr, ill. II. Title.
QC931.4 .S48 2003
551.51'8—dc21

                                                    2003004702

Table of Contents

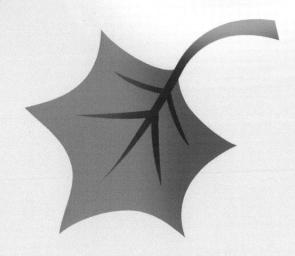

Whoosh! The wind sweeps in.
Leaves and hats go flying.

Where does wind begin?

5

How Wind Begins

Wind can begin in mountains or valleys, oceans or forests. Wind begins where warm and cool air meet.

Warm and Cool Air

Oceans and land heat up during the day and cool down at night.

Warm air expands, and cool air shrinks. As air warms and cools, it rises and falls, sinks and stirs. Wind is born.

Global Winds

Global winds are powerful streams of air.
They blow steadily over large parts of the world.

Twirl around on your tiptoes. Feel the air rush past your face and fingers. The earth spins every day, and global winds pass over the surface of the world.

Trade winds are one kind of global wind.
In the days when trading ships had huge sails
to help them move, the steady trade winds
swept them along on ocean highways.

12

Jet streams are long ribbons of powerful global winds. From six miles (10 kilometers) above us, they sweep over the world. They create a pathway for storms to follow.

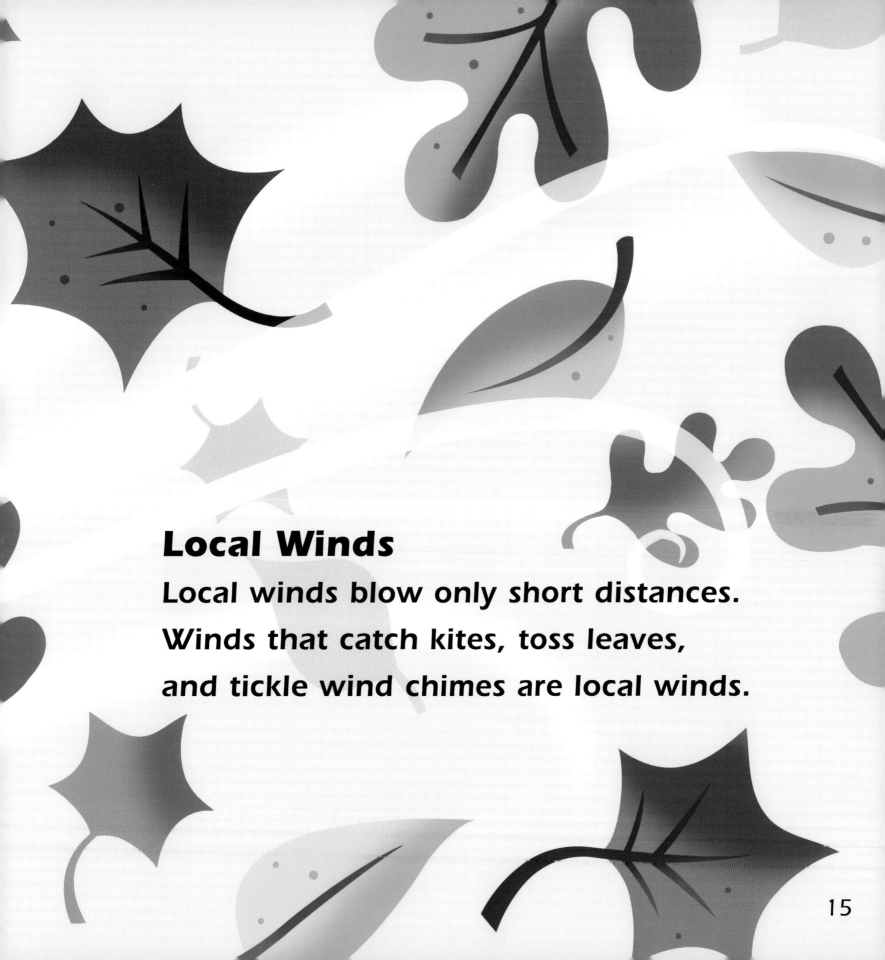

Local Winds

Local winds blow only short distances.
Winds that catch kites, toss leaves,
and tickle wind chimes are local winds.

Beach Breeze

People at the beach on a summer day
feel a cool breeze coming in from the water.

At night, the breeze on the beach changes direction. As the sun sets, the air over the land cools down faster than the air over the water. The air over the land sweeps out to replace the warmer, rising air over the water. People walking along the shore might feel a cool breeze blowing out toward the water.

Hurricanes and Tornadoes

A hurricane begins as a group of small thunderstorms that gets bunched together over the ocean. Hurricane winds can roar across islands and seashores at more than 150 miles (241 kilometers) per hour.

A tornado is
a spinning cloud
that comes down
toward the ground.
It can damage trees
and buildings as it
rips across the land.

Ride the Wind

Grab a pretty kite with a long string.

Find a large open area with nothing overhead.

Run into the field with your kite behind you.

Let your kite catch a breeze. Whoosh! Up it goes!

You Can Make a Tornado

What you need:

- two empty, two-liter plastic soda bottles
- water
- duct tape

What you do:

1. Make sure you have an adult help you.

2. Fill one of the bottles two-thirds full of water.

3. Fasten the two containers together using the duct tape. Be sure there are no places for water to leak from your bottles.

6. Turn the tornado maker over so the bottle holding the water is on top. Move the bottles in a circular motion.

7. Watch the tornado form in the top bottle as the water rushes into the bottom bottle.

Fast Facts

- Wind can be used to make energy. Windmills are used to catch the wind. When a windmill turns, the power of the windmill moves to a machine. Wind is a good source of energy because it is clean and will never run out.

- There are places in the world where the wind has a name. In Egypt, the desert wind is called khamsin. In western Australia, a wind that spins up from the ground and picks up small objects is called Cockeyed Bob. In Italy, a warm, south wind is called sirocco.

- When the weather turns cold, a measurement called windchill tells you how cold it feels outside. Windchill is a combination of temperature and wind speed. Even if the temperature is not below freezing, windchill can make it feel as if it is.

- There are many fun sports that are perfect for a windy day. Sailing, windsurfing, and kite flying are some sports that would not be possible without wind.

Glossary

breeze—a gentle wind

expand—to get bigger

global—something that exists throughout the world. When winds blow steadily over large parts of the earth, they are global.

hurricane—a dangerous, powerful storm. Hurricanes can damage cars, buildings, and other things in their path.

local—something that stays in a fairly small area

temperature—how hot or cold something is

tornado—a windstorm with a funnel-shaped cloud

To Learn More

At the Library

Dorros, Arthur. Feel the Wind. New York: Crowell, 1989.

Fowler, Allan. Can You See the Wind? New York: Children's Press, 1999.

Schaefer, Lola M. A Windy Day. Mankato, Minn.: Pebble Books, 2000.

On the Web

Fact Hound offers a safe, fun way to find Web sites related to this book. All of the sites on Fact Hound have been researched by our staff. http://www.facthound.com

1. Visit the Fact Hound home page.
2. Enter a search word related to this book, or type in this special code: 1404800948.
3. Click on the FETCH IT button.

Your trusty Fact Hound will fetch the best sites for you!

Index